CALLING COLLECT

Calling Collect

POEMS BY
GERALD DUFF

A University of Central Florida Book
University Presses of Florida
Orlando

University of Central Florida – Contemporary Poetry Series

Other works in the series:

George Bogin: *In a Surf of Strangers*
Van K. Brock: *The Hard Essential Landscape*
Malcolm Glass: *Bone Love*
Susan Hartman: *Dumb Show*
David Posner: *The Sandpipers*
Nicholas Rinaldi: *We Have Lost Our Fathers*
Edmund Skellings: *Heart Attacks*
Edmund Skellings: *Face Value*
Robert Siegel: *In a Pig's Eye*

University Presses of Florida, the agency of the State of Florida's
university system for publication of scholarly and creative works,
operates under policies adopted by the Board of Regents. Its
offices are located at 15 Northwest 15th Street, Gainesville,
Florida 32603.

"A Ceremony of Light" appeared in *Sewanee Review* 82 (1974),
copyright University of the South.
"Marginal Note" appeared in *Ball State University Forum* 11 (1970),
which holds the international copyright.

Library of Congress Cataloging in Publication Data

Duff, Gerald.
    Calling collect.

    "A University of Central Florida book."
    I. Title.
PS3554.U3177C3   811'.54   82-2819
ISBN 0-8130-0711-9   AACR2

Acknowledgments

Some of these poems have appeared in the following
magazines and anthologies: *Aim, Ball State University
Forum, Florida Quarterly, Boston University Journal,
Folio, Green River Review, Hika, Hiram Poetry Review,
Jimson Weed, Kansas Quarterly, Laurel Review, Mississippi
Review, Moonshine Review, The Nation, National Forum,
New Southern Poets* , ed. Guy Owen and Mary C. Williams
(University of North Carolina Press, 1975), *Sewanee Review,
South Carolina Review, Starting with Poetry,* ed. Ann C.
Colley and Judith K. Moore (Harcourt, Brace, Jovanovich,
1973), *Strong Voice, Tar River Poetry, Versus, Southern
Poetry Review, St. Andrews Review.*

A selection of the poems has been published as *A Ceremony
of Light* in the Interim Press Chapbook Series in England.

For Audrey, Stuart and Susan

Contents

Calling Collect

What Would Stay Her

May Belle Holt, never married, fifty years
servant to her sister
has fallen with drink into a bed of fire ants.

Rosalie née Holt, twice widowed and twelve years
dying of a slow growth
cannot raise her.

She calls to the house for her blind brother
to help pull sister from the seething bed.

Sightless and fat he cannot do
what once he could.

May Belle lies quiet, drunk on wine
steadily stung by blood red beaks
and listens to song.

Rolling away from the hands of kin
she puts aside what would stay her.
She croons to the mindless jaws,
and on that final bed of fire
savors her fall.

Here Where I Am Able To Wake

Always in that dream
the woman who was my wife
is not at home, late again

It is night, quiet, I am living
in the North woods
the snow is deep, the air cold and cracked

At three in the night of the dream
she comes, with small noises
on a tall horse, black and wide

Her dress is uniform

She sits erect and silent
I come to the door of the cabin,
the moon full against the cold

and ask her in

She refuses
speaks in general terms
of my general failure
promises never to see me again
and rides slowly across the clearing
into the dark woods

Gerald Duff

I go back to bed in the cabin
and find myself easily asleep . . .

twice unconscious

there in that dream in the cabin
and here where I am able to wake . . .

A Country Grave

I've forgotten how to get there,
even though I spent three hours last October
driving back roads and dim cattle trails.
The roadside man didn't know either,
he coughed and bit into an apple
from a brown bag.
She made us promise, me especially
"not in those woods
don't bury me there,
they're all country people,
I'm not from there"
But I was just married and
father said "seventy dollars."
He didn't remember when I asked him last month—
six years after and still no tombstone.

But at the grave foot is a metal marker
so bright you have to view it
at an angle to read the letters.

Gerald Duff

A History of Windows

By water late in the century
his sentence completed
the convicted man writes a history of windows.
After the years in prison
where walks are dreamed into thousand-mile marches
and hearing sharpened into knives
he wants to comprehend the point
where the outside comes in.
He writes to record how light leaks out
and how darkness will float
through any carpentered gap.

Marginal Note

In yesterday's seminar you gave a paper
on Wordsworth's use of caesura in The Prelude, Book II,
standing quiet and scholarly
plucking only once at the necklace around your throat
boring your classmates
and especially me, your teacher,
whose duty is to appreciate caesura
and The Prelude, Book II.
I gave you an A, of course,
because of the close attention to form
and because of the sureness of your speech.
"Thorough and exacting," I wrote
at the bottom of the last page
fixing you as a mind quite promising and quick.
So today as I walked past the grass court
and saw you playing tennis with a sweating boy
I thought of Wordsworth, the uses of caesura
and the brown mole on your left thigh.

Gerald Duff

Getting by the Town Madman

He comes up
out of the ditch, roaring,
coins tongued against his teeth,
slaver down his chin.

No matter where we run
he fronts us,
contains our hopeless dodges,
closes in.
He has us
between scabbed hands
and lifts us up to kiss
his bellowing cheek.

Schooled by that touch
we are saved, set free
and ever afterwards
live a useful life.

We All Have Dreams

Found in "Ask the Doctor,"
Mt. Vernon, Ohio, *News*

Doctor
all my girlfriends dream
They say they dream neat things
and they enjoy their experience of dream

I have never dreamed
and I am losing out
in not having a neat experience of dream
I have asked people
and they all claim dreams.

Is there some way
I can learn to dream?

Brenda
everyone dreams
even you. In your case
you don't remember dreaming,
therefore you think
you don't dream.

The human dream lasts
about two hours.
Most have two to four experiences of dream
each night.

Gerald Duff

There are ways
of remembering dreams
but I can't assist you
beyond these words.

My Lost Children

I ask myself,
what does the image of my lost children
playing in a hammock mean?

Their fingers and toes twine in cords
so that as the hammock flips over they hang
like possums waiting for resurrection.

They do not notice their dark visiting father
heavy in his skin and his smiles
sitting near them in a ladder-backed chair.

The spears of light through the pine needles
make no patterns
on the grass for them.

A bird in the swaying branches above
is a flash of red
not a cardinal announcing the Spring.

The day is warm, they like the dizziness,
the scrape of needles against their backs
the turning of the earth and trees.

Gerald Duff

What they feel is not love or loss
but knotted cord, rope burn and vertigo
as the landscape spins.

They laugh, they gasp, they utter cries
of no design, of no point
of no motive at all.

"See me," they call. "See me spin."
"Watch everything turn."

The Bluff

For Vereen Bell

And we are here
on the bluff
above the water of Lake Burton,
a long-buried city somewhere beneath us
fish swimming in its streets.

In the anchored boat below our height
our sons wait
watching their fathers.

In turn each of us will grip the steel hand-hold
wired to the strand of cable
connected to the tree above.

When my time comes
I need only let myself go
to feel the water pull me to it.

Swinging out over the lake
the eyes of my son upon me
I must at that true moment
let myself cease all holding
and come in a fall to the water.

14   Gerald Duff

For my son I enter the water
with no struggle
my fingertips touching above my head
and slide away from the sun and the air
deep into the cool and the darkness
down where the light dims and bones give
where my movements slow into dance
where my weight finds its true balance.

The city hidden in the belly of the lake invites me
but I have earned the right of refusal.
I have paid my way back
to the surface
and the bluff rising there above me.

While I crawl from the hold of the water
it is your time to leave the bluff
as our sons watch their fathers perform.

Heavier than ever before
I rest at the edge of the water,
taken by the concentric circles
that radiate to the shore.

Calling on Old Lovers

Always their hair is changed—
shorter, generally
with more curl

They are more substantial
browner, healthy
more given to talk

they are employed—
practical, involved.

As they shower while you sit with a drink
(they always shower while you sit with a drink)
you look at familiar objects
moved into a new city:
a bed, a mirror, a book.

Then while the water runs and drains away
you feel yourself
needing to leave
you rise just as they emerge from the shower
wet, dripping, wrapped in a towel,
clean

Gerald Duff

You embrace and kiss in obligation
lips tractionless, different,
rubbery now somehow
And you're finding your own way out
after promises to call,
to keep in touch

The door closes behind you like syrup.

Below in a rented car
you clear your wallet of old pictures,
breathing normally, as you feel the water
on your shirtfront prickle and dry.

Divorce

Sleeping in a separate bed
I wake to glass breaking.
Something outside is coming in
to seek out what's left.
Roused, I offer it the typewriter,
a vase of flowers, my undying respect.
Refusing all I have, it picks one apple
from a bowl of artificial fruit
and shambles off down the street.
I go back to bed alone:
the night air from the broken window is sweet.

Gerald Duff

The New Teacher of American Literature
Charts a Course

In my office there is quiet
I study Puritan theology
I ready myself to teach

My children do not live with me
I study accounts of early settlers
I ready myself to teach

The woman I love is not with me
I study the journals of merchants
I ready myself to teach

My course is American
I study expectation and loss
I ready myself to teach

History

Late in the day after the world war.
The abandoned hole was a Standard well
left from the thirties with its breadlines and gangsters,
a dry hole with dead snakes
at bottom.

The rotted covering gave way beneath you
and the crumbling earth let you down.
You slid into a dry mouth.
What you had lived on
you live wedged in.

But look up.

They'll sink parallel shafts
begin to pump air
lower food by rope
drip water through tubes.

Reporters will gather.
The country will notice and work overtime.
At noon you'll see a perfect circle
of light directly above
and at midnight the stars.

Gerald Duff

The last remarks will be the same:
gone into the ground alive will come out dead
and be made ready to go into the ground.
There will be cheers and groans.
Look up.
The worst has already happened.

Among the Newly Moulted

For Susan

Reclining on a sofa our host taunts us,
newly met,
into the outdoors of his party.

He directs us to wander outside
to follow the smell of honeysuckle
until we come to a far fence

Laughing, we begin to parody courtship—
hold hands, smile, simper—

We can afford to leave no feeling unmocked
we have learned more than enough
all that we believe left to us
are consciously worn words and moves
mouthed and gestured a thousand times before.

Outside the screens of the lighted house
locusts are using this night
to come forth from years of burial
to shed hard yellowed skins, leaving old ways
and mount any support—
porch beams, trees, water pipes
the pants cuffs of drunken party-goers,
puzzled in the warm night—
to reach a place to mate with their kind.

Gerald Duff

We stop to study this working in the middle of night
to poke at the pale crawling bodies
seized in a cycle of such clumsy delay

lingering until the host inside repeats his mock command.

Rising we nearly touch
and begin to walk toward the smell of honeysuckle
at the far fence
stepping carefully among the newly moulted.

Calling Collect

When my father calls me
from where he has moved—
from the house in the West at the edge
of the woods—
his sisters cluster around him
taking turns at the receiver
complaining proudly about sons who never visit
who two weeks of each year
preach revivals somewhere in the middle of the country
bring baptism and the good news.

"Pray," each croons, "pray for me.
I'm holding on. The doctor won't say.
Today I fell,
Outside in the yard by the ash tree.
Here all the children are sick.
Your father won't say, but oh
he doesn't feel right.
Pray. Listen, listen.
Listen to me."

Hearing I answer my kin.
I shout, clear my throat, speak distinctly.
but still I can't say words
that they can hear.

Gerald Duff

The connection is fuzzy, echoing, weak.
I think the lines are breaking down.
But still they call. They speak.
They tell me who I am.

On the Day Roger Maris Hit His
Sixty-first Home Run

For D. J. D.

It is the fall of the year 1961
On the screen before us
Roger Maris hits his sixty-first home run.

In your throat cancer growls for outlet.

You will not last
they have told me
your skin glows yellow
like the Louisville slugger Maris swings.

It is the liver's failure, they say,
behind the yellow
and the bloat of the belly,
the revolution in the self.

Now I am leaving your room forever.
Your eyes, huge as zeros in your head,
try now to hold me,
your newly married son.
Their image carries
as I walk from the darkness of that room.

Behind me in color on a screen
the Yankees win the pennant.

Each fan in that distant city roars.

Gerald Duff

Privileged Looks

Always a clock rimmed by a glowing circle
hangs above an exit
no one ever takes.

Though the promises are never kept,
the privileged looks into the future always lies,
we return to wait for the light
to dim and give us the darkness.
Around us mourn the well-dressed solitary men
who leave in the middle of things
checking their wrists.

We know nothing more pitiable than the blankness
of an unlit screen.
We look away from it,
the way husbands and wives move apart in bed
to sleep back to back
the way the winner in his guilt quits his game.

We hurry to leave before the act is complete,
before a sunset, an embrace
the shoes bouncing against the pavement behind a car,
the long shot of the city or the hanging man.

The Conventional Blind Pianist

The conventional blind pianist
like the conventional white dog,
dead on every roadway of every journey,
does not create himself.
He fulfills a design,
realizes a form
as water freezes into crystals
and as planets wheel around suns.

At the end of each number
rising to stand near his bench, he
is encircled by the considerate arm
of the M. C. pointing him toward the proper camera.
Dead eyes blinking, the pianist
smiles and waves, secure in his belief
that he supports some thesis.

Gerald Duff

We cough and blink as the credits roll up behind us.
We come out of the darkness
and stare down at the concrete.
Unspeaking we scatter into the intermissions we never ask.
We cannot meet the eyes in the line
forming in the street.

Welding

For Terry Bradshaw,
quarterback and welder

"I could be happy just welding,"
you said sitting in the dressing room after practice
after the exercise in form for form's sake.
Looking about you at your teammates
you confided in us,
fellow Southerners in the Steel City,
your pleasure in fusing things together.

In your off-seasons away from the measured boundaries,
the lined plots of ground where all patterns threaten
    to fly apart,
you seek a difference—
in Grand Cane in North Louisiana
where there is no telephone,
no outside line calling signals.
There you bend to your work
establish an electrical connection
strike an arc
and weave a thin web of steel between parts
making one thing from many.
Away from stunts, traps, fumbles, incompletions
you find yourself separate and together
bringing things steadily into balance
far from the perilous fragments of your Sunday afternoons.

          Gerald Duff

Certain Fish Confined

The threat is over.
The signs are good.
Clarius Betrachus is confined
to an area south of the marshes.

Poisons, hounds, and prayer
had failed. Air
itself proved no barrier,
nor woods, nor flame, nor fence.

Defeat, unexpected, come through over
extension and poor lines of communique.
Advance parties were benumbed
without chance of warning

incoming groups. Two hundred thousand
died in one small pool.
Forty thousand three hundred and two
littered one stretch of road

with hard, slick, grayish hides. Morning
readers chuckle, while the few remaining
to the South lie silent now, burrowing deeper
into the walls of canals, awaiting the next
    sunspot, tremor, mutation.

The Death of Miss Annie Elam

"It should serve," stated the chairman of Labor,
"as a lesson to all who work with fuel."

The driver of the earth-mover, bored—
thinking of the night to come
with its beer and friends
lets slip the clutch
too soon.

The pipe gives, pulls away from connection—
a sudden seepage of gas into the house
across the linoleum and rug-covered floors
until an instant marriage/divorce
with the flame of a Christmas candle.

The woman who lives inside, reading—
the retired teacher of English, spinster,
veteran of forty-seven years of recitations
of Bryant's "Thanatopsis" and Chaucer's Prologue
to the *Canterbury Tales*
is lifted, changed, loved.

Gerald Duff

Her house opens like a model of Shakespeare's Globe
yields up the groundlings inside
tosses its clothes, certificates of merit and service,
senior class play bills, graded compositions,
framed appreciations, unpublished poems
to the limbs of the waiting trees—

. . . bare ruin'd choirs where late the sweet birds sang . . .

She hears
She is lessoned
made bride
to the airy bones
of her favorite line.

With Friends at Franklin Cemetery

We went, along with our wives
and children, to see the stones
Allen Tate put in his ode
about radiations from soldier bones.

Beer cans, wine bottles, Trojans
guarded the fence of mock quartz
made in Texas and purchased
by fat ladies doing their parts

for grandfathers who soiled
their pants at the first shot
and then, remembering, marched through the creek
to give up all in one plot

of green, maintained now by Yazoo.
Our families, chilled, stayed
in the car and called, "no pictures,
the light's beginning to fade."

Gerald Duff

Projection for April

I sat in a wheelbarrow all summer
feeling the grass grow over the hubs
and across the handles.
By September I have moved twice—
once to scratch my left earlobe and
once to wave to Molly.
I descended on Columbus Day and
with much tearing of bermuda strands
pushed my throne into a shed.
There's a white spot left on the lawn
which will be invisible after the first
snow falls
but I predict rebirth by April.

At the Flood

Flares burn warning at all the approaches.
The air is filled with the river,
the river filled with earth.

In the rising brown water
my feet are steadily cut from under me.
It is my hold on my parents' hands
that keeps me from sliding away with the current.

It is the time I live alone
disguised in childhood.

We go to see the bridge that is prying itself
away from its banks and its highway
its pontoons turning their bellies
to the black birds in the air.

Death is the dance of the headless chicken
which my mother causes with a hand's quick motion
behind the willows of the yard.

It is the clump my father's flashlight picks out
in the darkness
where the mule was gored by the bull.

Gerald Duff

Now my parents, young beside me, edge nearer
the bridge in flood
but I drag, fall, scream
to spoil their view of the quick channel
afraid they want to know the powers of rushing water.

Hearing my own cries
how can I tell them with words
what the water takes me to know:
the years of his blindness to come,
her long wasting into the yellow of the chicken's claw?

A Convention of the Sleepless

They move from darkness into light
since the darkness they want is denied them.

They come together to be with others
wanting relief from being with others.

They drive backroads no one travels at night.
The theaters they pass are closed, the drugstores unlit.

They deserve the pity of sleepers:

For the radio's glow, the clock tick, the other
always to be only itself
never dreamed into a new life,
no dark conversions.

Ever to listen to the pulse crawl against the pillow.
To live on the boundaries of sleep.
To hear each syllable of all that's said.
To have destinations.
To greet the light daily as an old friend.

Gerald Duff

From the suburbs, from the dark farms
from the flickering rooms of home
they come to the city's limits.

Each one of them can never forget
someone else is there.
Each one always knows
he is himself.

The Deep Breather

Taking deep breaths rapidly,
stiffening the stomach muscles—
    black-out . . .

Children learning the process
by accident make it a rite—
dots before the eyes . . .

the horizon swooping up
vanishing . . .
and instantly, it seems to the breather,

things righting themselves
and he's sitting on the ground
shaking his head

watching the dots melt.
The children who saw
his eyes roll back

and who pinched him cruelly
to no response
always laugh when he returns

                    Gerald Duff

and ask him how it was.
The deep breather
can never answer

except to stare at the earth
and shake his head, while
smiling a slow, soft smile.

Honey Island

On the day of the night of our commencement
we came away from the coastal plain
and turned for Honey Island.

We came to the place we hunted,
the only high ground in the swamp
the mound where the last century's rebel deserters left
the sweetness bees had gathered from flowers
in trade for cured bacon and thread and knives.

We drove in smoking cars away from the open Gulf
our only stop for oil for the burnt-out engines.
We drove away from the sun
and we sank ourselves in pine thickets.

We came to dance with unknown women
under a galvanized shed at the edge of the woods.
We came for the sound of the artesian spring
gushing its water forever
and the cry of the black singer begging
for all the love he'd lost.

We came to place our arms about the bodies of women
and feel the sweat start with music through their clothes.

Gerald Duff

We came to a hill of earth
where the diamondback rattler suns
and the swamp's last panther screams
like a woman in the night.

We came to swim in the cold water
and to drink the bright whiskey.

We came to the high ground of Honey Island
to begin that day our fall into history.

Documentary

Just at dark my dog Beastie
(wearing a new collar) startled me

by catching a half-grown bird learning to fly.
I heard the parents' alarm cry

and went outside to watch
the bird flapping between the paws, no match

for the dog's mumbling attack.
I questioned whether to turn back

or to rescue, but remembering a poem by Tennyson
certain documentaries on Africa, a paper done

in an undergraduate course on evolutionary theory,
thought it best not to disturb a mystery.

The older birds swirled and dove
at the teeth mumbling and drooling above

the feathers. "One must be natural," I thought
and went inside to eat the steak I had bought.

Gerald Duff

Cottonmouth

Along the creek
near the shallow puddles
are signs left by a cottonmouth
indented, damp, and faint.
When I come this way
I kneel to see the patterns
poison has made,
designs formed
by a trailed stick
held by a boy
or by a trickle from the stream.
But, leaning closer,
I blink to see the skin.

Uncle Drunk, Mother Laughing

Uncle Drunk stuffed in the chair with his stuffed rabbit
sits singing
"Losing weight, losing weight, coming down, O Lord."

Mother will not laugh, looks down
hides her teeth with a hand.
I poke his arm, the rag-doll offer
he pushes away, cursing sweetly.

He tries to roll a cigarette, coughs
and drops his rabbit.
Mother slips away, laughing.
I'm there in the room, warm
smelling the pork fry.

O then, O that time.
Won't come back.
It's drafty
and I'm cold in my office.

Mother, listen to me and look up here.
Those stubbed butts can be cleaned up
and Uncle Drunk, singing, doesn't really mean it.

Gerald Duff

Cerne Abbas: Joining the Giant

On a chalk hillside in Dorset survives the giant
figure of a Stone Age warrior. No one knows
which people carved it, nor their reason.

Crossing these boundaries in the half-light
you can be slow: the outline's prehistoric.
High above the farms and abbey
you come to the last fence.
Stop to look:
it's the last sense
of the body you can have.

At the shape's center
the lines, angles, stones
the giant's hand
change you into what the town
across the mile of empty air
can see in the sun:
something dark moving at dawn toward a plan.

In a design you look down
to see the trail you've made.
Before you the sunlight carves the pattern
of all you've come to.
You move in that light the distance dimmed:
you become where you stand.

A Ceremony of Light

For Bernadine and Elizabeth Clark
Photographed on Christmas Day, 1912

On that morning in 1912
your father did what he could
against the darkness around you.

He lifted the oil lamp high
to illumine you
to take your image on Christmas of that year.

There you sit at attention—
gifts forgotten in a ceremony of light.

The light of that day is given back
by the tree above you.
The slow closing of the shutter
allowed a tracing of the movement
of the light.

The only moving arc in that frame
is a curve in time,
a smear of light.

You show us what you were:
two children, dazzled beneath the splendid tree
sisters in the path of light.

Gerald Duff

Amazed, you became part
of what we shall never have:
the record of a movement
in a moment of your lives—
the faithful tracing of a hand's
moving of the source of light.

Seeing you now,
we give you all we can—
our close study,
the eyes behind our eyes,
our love for the movement of the light.

Trophy Room

As he stands in his green suit
the great tusk leans before him
burning in the growing dark.

About him the animals
crouch in stillness and stealth
eyes glowing, unblinking, fixed.

In this place he must move with care
feet placed precisely on the path
between the beasts.

The hair on his forearm brushes against the tail of the wolf
his breath stirs the mane of the lion
his finger traces veins in the ear of the elephant
In the dark his feet become the path.

He listens, he can hear himself fading from the page.

Gerald Duff

A Law of Motion

Uniformed, numbered, praying
I drop to my knees
in an outdoor chapel
and study two ants
mastering summer's last crumb.

Somewhere away from here
deer browse in soft grass,
nose deeply into cold water.

I come to know my life.

The long fall through space
the air growing warmer
one frame in focus
before the stop

Physicists swear the earth itself
is attracted to each body.

The deer turns, looks back once.
Becomes the foliage.

A Day for Hearts

When you pass the mirror you catch yourself
pushing back your hair
to further the self you want to see.
You learn to love what's deserving.

Know it this way:
on a day for hearts
you ask if you are loved
and get the answer you need:
the yes from a self that loves a self
it thinks it's earned.

Here is what you come for:
the self you think you are
and the self a mother dreams.

Gerald Duff

A Far-Off Animal Sound

Old blind father
ten years ago you wanted to live
with me.
I said no
thinking to nurse a marriage
headed then toward the death
it was to earn.

There you stayed.

Listen, I remember, a child, hunting with you
running to follow the voices of hounds.
Then I chased you through gulleys
slow bayous, wide fields of thorns, gray undergrowth,
the spotty clearings of ruined homesteads.
Green limbs snapped back into my weeping face
and clawed at my good eye
until I begged you to wait for me.

You would stop, intent, your face
lifted to a far-off animal sound,
your eyes asking if I heard too.

Then, old blind father
you turned, you plunged
you vanished
into the trees.

Wife

In a dream of many women
the woman who will be his wife
walks down a model runway.

Her robe opens with each step
to glimpses of white beneath.

The master of ceremonies calls her lovely
remarks on the art of her gown
admires her coloring against the background of white
and asks her to lift the chin to a graceful angle.

She obeys what another man tells her.

He sits at the end of the room
in a wall of jungle plants in vases.
His hands open and close in fever.
There are sounds of middle-aged women.

The future nears the end of the runway,
and its eyes show no promise or fear.

She returns to the stage where parading begins
swaying slightly with the unstable footing
the gown opening and closing in rhythm.

Gerald Duff

He blinks will-less as she abandons
the space of the room to him.
He hates her
and he will love her
forever.

The Flies

In the Alps the blue air of summer
lies about us,
clear water breathes at our feet.

My son, at thirteen, a child
whose body now blooms blondly with hair
amuses himself with flies that pester the swimmer.
He makes a game of their buzzing sorties,
smiles as they crawl over his face and chest.
He commands them
calls them his troops and gesturing a charge
falls into the pool
taking all with him.

Behind us across the valley climbers of a rock face
move with care to order where they stand,
then trust themselves to nylon cord
in a long suspension over a mile of space.
Swinging out over nothing they hear
only their rope support sing in its stays.

Before me beneath the plane of water
my sons sinks into the shadow rising from the depths
to meet him.
In a burst
the flies break from the water's surface
and turn in a drone for me.

Gerald Duff

Tracking

Leave the clearing
follow the trail of animals,
the seep and flow of water.

Sink into thicket.

    Here always bowels yearn
    hands are chapped with water or cold
    nails worn down with stone
    hair tangled with briars
    teeth set on edge

Find solid ground
a time to darken,
to quiet the breathing
to listen to the coded language
of leaf and tissue

Here is where you begin—
    within earth
    and without

Sleeping in the Jungle Hammock

Away from home for the first time
I lay each night apart from the others,
the ones praying in the lighted tent
in the fever swamp.

It's a kinsman, maybe, who has paid my way there
because the woods are good for a boy.
He sings praises with a friend, a brother scout of the eagle
a fellow student of the Lord.

They are praying now in the long hours
after midnight
their voices bright, lifted, grieving in joy
as they ask the dark air
its blessing of the other.

They kneel, names together, they witness,
shadows thrown and moving
on a lighted cloth wall.

I lie alone beyond the rim of light
raised above the earth
away from whatever crawls
in the dead night of childhood,
witness to the evidence of things not seen.

Gerald Duff

Lying in the dark
the water of an unnamed stream
flowing steady beside me toward a later time
I listen for the sound of a master, the ruler
of the fever swamp, the dark hunter
I know I am never to hear.

A Picture of Belief

Coming this way
the man in the white suit has turned
to look back into history,
those tire tracks swerving in the smooth dust.

Ahead of him the wreck, tilted off balance
one wheel sheared off
where it nosed into the barrier.
The women are turned away,
one comforts the other—
hand to her eyes, her dress plaid
the ribbon in the hair matching.

Nearest, the suspicious man in the foreground
carefully leans against the flaking fence,
cap low over his face
shaded against the sun
and studies us,
looking hard into the closing lens
where he knows some future
will surely find him out.

Gerald Duff

photo by Dan Mayfield

Gerald Duff, vice-president and dean of the college of Southeastern at Memphis, has previously taught literature at Vanderbilt, Kenyon, and the University of Exeter. In addition to his scholarly books and articles on English Romantic writers, he has published in England a chapbook of his poetry, *A Ceremony of Light*. His poems have appeared in *The Nation, Sewanee Review,* and many other journals, as well as in anthologies of contemporary verse, such as *New Southern Poets*.